ECONOMY

THE SELF-DENYING DEPOSITOR

AND

PRUDENT PAYMASTER

AT THE

BANK OF THRIFT

By ORISON SWETT MARDEN

Author of
"PUSHING TO THE FRONT," "SECRET OF ACHIEVEMENT,"
"TALKS WITH GREAT WORKERS," ETC.

With the assistance of
ARTHUR W. BROWN

New York
THOMAS Y. CROWELL CO., PUBLISHERS

Kessinger Publishing's Rare Mystical Reprints

THOUSANDS OF SCARCE BOOKS ON THESE AND OTHER SUBJECTS:

Freemasonry * Akashic * Alchemy * Alternative Health * Ancient Civilizations * Anthroposophy * Astrology * Astronomy * Aura * Bible Study * Cabalah * Cartomancy * Chakras * Clairvoyance * Comparative Religions * Divination * Druids * Eastern Thought * Egyptology * Esoterism * Essenes * Etheric * ESP * Gnosticism * Great White Brotherhood * Hermetics * Kabalah * Karma * Knights Templar * Kundalini * Magic * Meditation * Mediumship * Mesmerism * Metaphysics * Mithraism * Mystery Schools * Mysticism * Mythology * Numerology * Occultism * Palmistry * Pantheism * Parapsychology * Philosophy * Prosperity * Psychokinesis * Psychology * Pyramids * Qabalah * Reincarnation * Rosicrucian * Sacred Geometry * Secret Rituals * Secret Societies * Spiritism * Symbolism * Tarot * Telepathy * Theosophy * Transcendentalism * Upanishads * Vedanta * Wisdom * Yoga * *Plus Much More!*

DOWNLOAD A FREE CATALOG AND SEARCH OUR TITLES AT:

www.kessinger.net

RUSSELL SAGE,
Capitalist.

b. Shenandoah, N.Y., Aug. 4, 1816.

Copyright, 1901,
By Thomas Y. Crowell & Company.
Tenth Thousand

ECONOMY.

As I sat at the café, I said to myself:
"They may talk as they please about what they call pelf,
They may sneer as they like about eating and drinking,
But help it I cannot, I cannot help thinking
How pleasant it is to have money, heigh-ho;
How pleasant it is to have money!"
Arthur Hugh Clough.

But for money and the need of it, there would not be half the friendship that there is in the world. It is powerful for good, if divinely used. — *George MacDonald.*

How beauteous are rouleaus! how charming chests
Containing ingots, bags of dollars, coins
(Not of old victors, all whose heads and crests
Weigh not the thin ore where their visage shines,
But) of fine unclipped gold, where dully rests
Some likeness, which the glittering cirque confines,
Of modern, reigning, sterling, stupid stamp; —
Yes! ready money is Aladdin's lamp.
Byron.

Whatever be your talents, whatever be your prospects, never speculate away on a chance of a palace that which you may need as a provision against the workhouse. — *Bulwer.*

The man who builds and wants wherewith to pay,
Provides himself a home from which to run away.
Young.

"Here it was that I experienced most of the hardships of my life," said Edward Moran, the eminent marine and figure painter, during a recent visit to Philadelphia. "I came from Lancashire, England, to New York, in the steerage of an immigrant ship. That was in 1844, when I was only fifteen years old. After stopping in the metropolis long enough to spend all my money, I walked to Philadelphia, doing chores for my board from town to town. Soon after I reached my destination, I began to study art under James Hamilton, to whom I owe much. Of course he could not understand my poverty, for I managed to present the air of one in comfortable circumstances; but one day he learned that I lodged in an attic room, and that my only furniture was a wooden chair and a copy of a New York newspaper.

"'How do you manage to get along?' he asked, in surprise.

"'Why,' I replied, 'I sleep on the newspaper at night, and sit on the chair in the daytime.'"

This is an extreme case, but it is typical of the early frugality of thousands who have risen from poverty and ignorance to fame and fortune. Indeed, so common have youthful struggles with hardship been in America that an English tourist named birth in a log cabin and pinching poverty as necessary preparatives for future greatness here. Of course we all know that our country has passed the log-cabin stage in its development, but it still holds true, and always will, that a boy who is willing to deny himself in order to improve himself will rise in the world. He may not, like Moran, become a successful exhibitor in the galleries of London and Paris, associate of the National Academy, and member of the American Water Color Society and of the Pennsylvania Academy of Fine Arts; but, in his own sphere and in his own way, he is sure to grow into a larger life because of his sacrifices.

"I will give five pounds toward the expenses of the city mission," said a Scotchman, without solicitation, to a clergyman whom he met on the street.

"Thank you," exclaimed the clergyman, earnestly; "the money is greatly needed, and will do a deal of good."

"I wonder," he mused, as he left the other, "how so close a man happens to be so generous, of his own accord!"

"Wait a minute," said the Scotchman, who had turned to follow the minister. "I have the five pounds about me, and I may as well give it now as send it; it will save a postage stamp."

The trait which led him to avoid using an unnecessary postage stamp had ruled all his business transactions and enabled him to give the five pounds which the clergyman had not thought of receiving from so "close" a man.

"We shan't get much here," whispered a lady to her companion, as John Murray blew out one of the two candles by whose light he had been writing when they asked him to contribute to some benevolent object. He listened to their story and gave one hundred dollars. "Mr. Murray, I am very agreeably surprised," said the lady quoted; "I did not expect to get a cent from you." The old Quaker asked the reason for her opinion; and, when told, said, "That, ladies, is the reason I am able to let you have the hundred dollars. It is by practicing economy that I save up money with which to do charitable actions. One candle is enough to talk by."

Emerson relates the following anecdote: "An opulent merchant in Boston was called on by a friend in behalf of a charity. At that time he was admonishing his clerk for using whole wafers instead of halves; his friend thought the circumstance unpropitious; but to his surprise, on listening to the appeal, the merchant subscribed five hundred dollars. The applicant expressed his astonishment that any person who was so particular about half a wafer should present five hundred dollars to a charity; but the merchant said, 'It is by saving half-wafers, and attending to such little things, that I have now something to give.'"

FOUNDATION STONES OF FORTUNE.

"New England has been noted for its poor soil and hard conditions generally," says J. G. Holland, "yet there is no other spot on the face of the earth that contains so much comfort to the square mile. Every man born on New England soil tries and expects to better his condition during his life, and he goes to work at the beginning with the end definitely in view. The rich men of New England are men who began their prosperity with humble savings. Whatever their income was, they did not use it all. Twenty-five or fifty dollars a year was considered worth saving and laying by. A fortune acquired in this way was cohesive, strong, and permanent."

A. M. Gow tells of a young Englishman who came to America for the purpose of making it his home.

He was a miner, and, for the purpose of finding employment, sought the coal mines of Western Pennsylvania. He was uneducated, but was determined, by the help of his thrifty wife, to win the esteem and confidence of his neighbors by his industry and frugality. He rented with his house a small piece of ground, which he and his wife, when he was not employed in his mine, worked together as a garden and potato-patch. He was a man of good habits, wasting neither his time nor his money in bad company or foolish amusements. He could not afford to be idle; so, when by accident his arm was broken and he could not work in the mine, he went into a harvest-field and raked hay with one hand for twenty-five cents a day. When wages were high, he saved his money; when wages were low, he thought it fortunate when he could pay expenses. Thus, by habits of honest labor and economy, he contrived to save enough money in the course of several years to buy a fine farm, where he lived in comfort, enjoying the confidence of his neighbors and the independence of a well-furnished home. It was a principle with him never to waste time when he could find work; never to quit work because he could not get the highest wages; never to drink spirits, and always to save his money. Of course, there were those who made fun of his hard work and economy, but he became able to point to his home and his farm as the result of his shrewdness, while they had nothing to show for their years of misspent time and wasted money.

"The first thing that a man should learn to do," says Andrew Carnegie, "is to save his money. By saving his money he promotes thrift,— the most valued of all habits. Thrift is the great fortune-maker. It draws the line between the savage and the civilized man. Thrift not only develops the fortune, but it develops also the man's character."

The "loose change" which many young men throw away carelessly, or worse, would often form the basis of a fortune and independence. The earnings of the people of the United States, rich and poor, old and young, male and female, amount to an average of less than fifty cents a day. But it is by economizing such savings that one must get his start in business. The man without a penny is practically helpless, from a business point of view, except so far as he can immediately utilize his powers of body and mind. Besides, when a man or woman is driven to the wall, the chance of goodness surviving self-respect and the loss of public esteem is frightfully diminished.

It is a lesson which every generation teaches anew, that it is they who are masters in little savings who become possessors of great or moderate fortunes. "Despise not the day of small things."

The next census of the United States will probably record a total population of one hundred million people. Were every one to save but a cent a day, the aggregate saving would be one million dollars a day, or three hundred and sixty-five millions a year. This total is large enough to affect the prosperity of the nation as a whole, and each one's share in it is sufficient to influence his individual prosperity. But think of the full significance of savings of two, five, ten, or twenty-five cents a day!

"I wish I could write all across the sky, in letters of gold," says Rev. William March, "the two words, 'savings bank.'"

School savings banks have been praised because they teach the pupils habits of thrift. The principal of a school in West Virginia calls attention to the fact that the plan has brought about a noticeable decrease in the amount of candy and gum consumed by the girls, and in the number of cigarettes smoked by the boys. "Evidently, therefore," says the "Youth's Companion," "the pupils are learning what thrift really means; that it is not merely saving money, but saving it by cutting off useless expenses and foregoing bad habits."

Teach children not to waste trifles, which they often throw away without thought, and which, if saved, might be of use to others if not to themselves. Wrapping paper, pieces of twine, odds and ends of various kinds, may do service a second time if put away until the need for them arises. The habit of economy is one that ought to be cultivated, for careful saving makes lavish giving possible. Hoarding is not a vice of childhood, nor should it be encouraged, but the wise husbanding of resources for future expenditure is a valuable lesson that cannot be learned too early. The time of many a business man is often too valuable to be spent in saving pins or pieces of twine, etc., but with children, and, indeed, the average adult, minute savings usually pay.

"It is an old and recognized maxim," says William Mathews, "that the only way to become and keep rich in worldly goods, or even independent, is to save odds and ends, shreds and parings, to keep exact accounts, and to steer clear of everything that savors, in the smallest degree, of waste. The sayings in the old school-books, about the importance of taking care of the pence, and 'a pin a day,' and 'willful waste that leads to woful want,' are as true to-day as when first published; and men get on, financially, in the world, or come to grief, as they obey or scorn these lessons. All experience shows that, to produce diligently, and to take care of the scraps and savings, is the infallible compound process for acquiring riches; and the latter half of the process contributes to the result not a whit less powerfully than the former.

"In almost all the cases where men have accumulated great fortunes, attention to margins and remnants has been the secret of their success. Wealth did not come to them in huge windfalls, overwhelming them with opulence, but by gradual acquisitions, and by saving, year after year, the loose money which other men squander. By economizing the little sums which the thoughtless and improvident man deems not worth looking after, — the pennies and dimes and quarter-dollars of which he keeps no reckoning, — the pyramid of their fortune has been slowly and surely reared."

Many people uselessly spend money because it is so "handy." Form a habit of depositing in the savings bank money which you do not immediately need, or, if you are not near a bank, in some place where it will be sure to remain unspent until you reach a bank.

" Lay by something for a rainy day," said a gentleman to an Irishman in his service. Not long afterwards he asked Patrick how much he had added to his store. " Faith, nothing at all," was the reply; " I did as you bid me, but it rained very hard yesterday, and it all went — in drink."

Evidently Patrick did not lay his money by in the proper place, a good savings bank.

Four years from the time Marshall Field left the rocky New England farm to seek his fortune in Chicago, he was admitted as a partner in the firm of Coaley, Farwell and Company. The only reason the modest young man gave, to explain his promotion, when he had neither backing, wealth, nor influence, was that he saved his money.

Benjamin Franklin said: "If you know how to spend less than you get, you have the philosopher's stone." Again he said: " Let honesty and industry be thy constant companions, and spend one penny less than thy clear gains; then shall thy pocket begin to thrive, creditors will not insult, nor want oppress, nor hunger bite, nor nakedness freeze thee."

Who does not feel honored by his relationship to Franklin, whether as a townsman or as a countryman, or even as belonging to the same race? Who does not feel a sort of personal complacency in regard to that frugality of his youth which laid the foundation for so much competence and generosity in his mature age; in that wise discrimination in his outlays, which held the culture of the soul in absolute supremacy over the pleasures of sense; and in that consummate mastership of the great art of living, which has carried his practical wisdom into every cottage in Christendom, and made his name immortal? Yet how few there are among us who would not disparage, nay, ridicule and condemn a young man who should follow Franklin's example!

"I knew one clerk who, at the age of twenty, (having then been at work eight years,) was receiving a salary of nine hundred dollars and saving nothing out of it," says William H. Maher. "He had an honest horror of debt, and intended that his account in the ledger should always show a small balance in his favor, but beyond this his idea of a salary was that it was just so much money that was his to spend each year. At the end of his twentieth year something led him to ask himself the question: 'What have you done with your salary this year?' He could make no answer. He thought upon the subject for several days, and finally took pencil and paper, determined to work out a reply. He had for the first time in his life become thoroughly interested in the matter of his expenses. He figured out that his board had cost about so much; clothes during the year about so much; he had sent his mother so much; his summer vacation had cost so much; and the total of these was about six hundred dollars. Could it be possible that he had spent three hundred dollars for amusement and trifles?

"He kept thinking over this and finally said to himself: 'Situated as I am, I ought to live on five hundred dollars, and I am going to do it next year. My salary will be one thousand dollars, and I ought to save half of it; I will try it, anyway.'

"He opened an account in a savings bank with a deposit of ten dollars, determining to deposit a like amount each week of the year. He knew that, if it should be necessary, he could draw out a little to help him over an emergency, but he was determined not to do this if it could possibly be avoided. He was surprised to see how much pleasure he had in watching his account grow; but far beyond this was the satisfaction in knowing that he was at length making definite preparations for the future. At the end of the year he had five hundred dollars in the bank. He had been to the theater but seldom; he had not been to any dances; but, looking back, it seemed to him to have been the pleasantest year of his life. He had made good use of the city library, and had extended his acquaintance into the homes of many pleasant people. His salary was increased, and his bank account had the benefit of it. In a few years there was a chance for him to get an interest in a good business, if he could get some help, and the men who endorsed for him were influenced by the sight of his bank-book, with the story it told of years of economy and good habits."

Many a young man, who has never considered the matter carefully, will find, on examination, that he is spending dollar after dollar to no particular purpose, and that a prompt, decided right-about-face is easily possible and will prove very satisfactory.

"A country recovers from hard times," says a writer on economics, "by an enormous aggregate of petty savings. While production is reasonably stationary, consumption varies. When men look twice at a cent before spending it, the country is growing richer, because more of what is produced is saved. From this fact comes another not usually accepted, but nevertheless true, that we grow rich more rapidly in 'hard times' than when business is active, and everybody seems to be making money."

This suggests that it is the disposition to save, even more than the amount of money in circulation, which measures the total of each savings-bank account.

An old bookkeeper says, in the "Youth's Companion," that it is surprising to see how many valuable things a man can buy if he simply economizes in little things.

"I once made up my mind that I would become the possessor of a gold watch. I saved up the money for it in this way: When I felt like eating a fifty-cent luncheon, as I often did, I ate a twenty-five-cent one instead, and put the other quarter aside for my watch fund. You will hardly believe it, but in less than six months I had saved money enough to purchase the watch."

"But you don't seem to have bought it," said his friend, observing that there were no outward signs of such a purchase.

"Well, no. When I found how easily I could get along without fifty-cent lunches, I concluded I could get along without the gold watch, and the watch fund is growing into a house-and-lot fund now."

A Kansas City newspaper publisher gave each of his newsboys a bank-book, at Christmas, showing that one dollar had been deposited to his credit in the bank. A promise was also made to deposit another dollar to the credit of each boy who should still have the original dollar in the bank six months later. There were one hundred boys in all. Fifty secured the additional dollar, some had increased it to ten or twelve dollars, and one boy had a total deposit of thirty-two dollars. On the next Christmas, one boy had nearly one hundred and fifty dollars in the bank. The president of the bank was so pleased with the result that he added another dollar, personally, to the account of every boy who had kept his deposit in a year. This was a very practical lesson in economy, and showed the possibility of saving, for few of the boys would have laid by a cent without this illustration of the power of pennies to make dollars.

HOW RICHES TAKE WINGS.

Buy what thou hast no need of, and ere long thou shalt sell thy necessaries. — *Franklin.*

We sacrifice to dress, till household joys and comforts cease. Dress drains our cellar dry, and keeps our larder lean; puts out our fires, and introduces hunger, frost, and woe, where peace and hospitality might reign. — *Cowper.*

A legend tells us of a master's apprentice, who, from the small bits of glass that had been thrown away, constructed a cathedral window of surpassing loveliness. The ideal held up before the boy's mind organized and brought together the broken bits, and wrought them into lines of perfect beauty. — *N. D. Hillis.*

When John W. McNalty, known as "Coal-oil Johnny," became suddenly rich, he was young and ignorant of business laws, and spent his money recklessly. He would buy a hack and a span of horses, and hire a man to drive for him; then, at the end of his ride, he would present the vehicle and the horses to the astonished driver. Such things soon made him poor again, and he had to work for his daily bread. His life had found its true level once more, like a river temporarily swollen by a sudden flood, which quickly subsides and keeps between its proper banks. Sooner or later, given good health and freedom from accidents, all men, or at least all families, gravitate to their natural financial level. They become wealthy and remain so only when and so long as they are fit to do so, according to the world's standard of fitness. The pressure of poverty or the desire to become independent induces industry and frugality, which in turn beget wealth; then abundance conduces to liberality, often to prodigality, and the hoarded treasures are surely scattered, whether slowly or swiftly. The old adage is usually true, that "it is but three generations from shirtsleeves to shirtsleeves;" and, even in the exceptional cases, the transition is measured by four or five generations only, at most.

The mad king, Ludwig of Bavaria, was reared without a practical idea of the value of money. As a minor he had very little spending money. When he became of age at eighteen, the State supplied him with a purse of gold. His first purchase was a locket for his mother. In paying for it, he handed the entire purse to the jeweler, saying, "Take what it is worth." How could he know the value of gold when he had never felt it? Then, when he wanted to make a Versailles out of a hunting park, or convert the sleepy Munich into a world-city, was it not natural that he should say to one, "Do what I bid!" and to another, "Pay what it costs!"

It is said that the Empress Josephine was allowed, at the beginning of her reign, $72,000 a year for her toilet, and that, later, this was increased to $90,000. But there was never a year during the time that she did not far overreach her allowance and oblige Napoleon to go to her relief.

According to the estimate Mason has made, Josephine spent, on an average, $220,000 yearly on her toilet, during her reign. It is only by going over her wardrobe article by article, and noting the cost and number of each kind of garment, that one can realize how a woman could spend this amount. Her hose, for instance, were almost always of white silk, often richly embroidered or in open work. She kept one hundred and fifty or more pairs on hand, and they cost from four dollars to eight dollars per pair.

She employed two hairdressers, — one for every day, at $1,200 a year; the other for great occasions, at $2,000 a year; and she paid them each from $1,000 to $2,000 a year for furnishings. It was the same for all the smaller items of her toilet.

But for the practical common-sense economy of Napoleon, the example of her extravagance would doubtless have spread like wildfire among the French nobility, and France would have shown, in the superlative degree, the sharp contrast of —

> "Wealth, a monster gorged
> 'Mid starving populations."

But nowhere and at no period were these contrasts more startling than in Imperial Rome. There a whole population might be trembling lest they should be starved by the delay of an Alexandrian corn-ship, while

PHINEAS T. BARNUM,
Great Manager of Tent Shows.

b. 1810; d. 1891.

the upper classes were squandering fortunes at a single banquet, drinking out of myrrhine and jeweled vases worth hundreds of pounds, and feasting on the brains of peacocks and the tongues of nightingales. As a consequence, disease was rife, and men were short-lived. At this time the dress of Roman ladies displayed an unheard-of splendor. The elder Pliny tells us that he himself saw Lollia Paulina dressed for a betrothal feast in a robe entirely covered with pearls and emeralds, which had cost 40,000,000 sesterces, and which was known to be less costly than some of her other dresses. Gluttony, caprice, extravagance, ostentation, impurity, rioted in the heart of a society which knew of no other means by which to break the monotony of its weariness or to alleviate the anguish of its despair.

The expense ridiculously bestowed on the Roman feasts almost passes belief. Suetonius mentions a supper given to Vitellius by his brother, in which, among other articles, there were two thousand of the choicest fishes, seven thousand of the most delicate birds, and one dish, from its size and capacity, named the ægis or shield of Minerva. It was filled chiefly with the livers of scari, a delicate species of fish, the brains of pheasants and peacocks, and the tongues of parrots, considered desirable chiefly because of their great cost.

Such things represent the extreme of lavishness, but in modern times, and in ways proportioned to their possessions, many rich people squander fortunes and many people of moderate means are unnecessarily liberal in some lines of expenditure.

"It absorbs the income of a province to bring up a baby," says a shrewd observer. "We riot in prodigality, and vie with each other in material accumulation and expense. Our thoughts are mainly on how to increase the products of the world, and how to get them into our own possession. The idea seems to be well-nigh universal that the millennium is to come by a great deal less work and a great deal more pay."

"It is easy to spend, but hard to keep money," says a modern economist. "Happiness is dependent upon the science of getting what one wants, or must have, out of what he receives, and preserving a margin, be it ever so small. For those who are secure in a regular income, such as many persons can obtain, this problem is sufficiently difficult, on account of the numberless contingencies, temptations, and demands over which one can exercise no foresight or control. For those who have no regular income the problem becomes one of almost impossible solution. It is said that humanity, considered as a whole, always lives within one year of starvation. Certain it is that only a very small portion of humanity is able to lay aside a whole year's income, or sufficient so that they can live through a year, spending only what they had previously earned, and laying up all their earnings for the current year. If this could be done, it would be a powerful aid in learning the science of spending.

"The science of spending is, in reality, the science of keeping. If one can keep, he may always have something to spend when occasion requires it. This science is learned most surely by acquiring the art of separating the essential from the non-essential objects of expenditure, satisfying the first fully, and the second only so far as can be done within the inexorable limits of the fund available."

"Men and women accustomed to gratify every whim

ECONOMY. 17

and caprice," says P. T. Barnum, " will find it hard, at first, to cut down their various unnecessary expenses, and will feel it a great self-denial to live in a smaller house than they have been accustomed to, with less expensive furniture, less company, less costly clothing, fewer servants, a smaller number of balls, parties, theater-goings, carriage-ridings, pleasure excursions, cigar-smokings, liquor-drinkings, and other extravagances; but, after all, if they will try the plan of laying by a 'nest-egg,' or, in other words, a small sum of money, at interest, or judiciously invested in land, they will be surprised at the pleasure to be derived from constantly adding to their little 'pile,' as well as from all the economical habits which are engendered by this course.

" The old suit of clothes, and the old bonnet and dress, will answer for another season; a cold bath and a brisk walk will prove more exhilarating than a ride in the finest coach; a social chat, an evening's reading with the family circle, or an hour's play at 'hunt the slipper' or 'blind man's buff,' will be far more pleasant than a fifty-dollar or a five-hundred-dollar party, when the reflection on the difference in cost is indulged in by those who begin to know the pleasures of saving. Thousands of men are kept poor, and tens of thousands are made so after they have acquired quite sufficient to support them well through life, in consequence of laying their plans of living on too broad a platform. Some families expend many hundreds or even many thousands of dollars yearly, while others secure more solid comfort and enjoyment, frequently, at one-twentieth as great an expense. Prosperity is a more severe ordeal than adversity, especially sudden prosperity. 'Easy come, easy go,' is an old and true proverb. A spirit of pride and vanity, when permitted to have full sway, is the undying canker worm which gnaws the very vitals of a man's worldly possessions, let them be small or great, hundreds or millions. Many persons, as they begin to prosper, immediately expand their ideas and commence expending for luxuries, until, in a short time, their expenses swallow up their income, and they become ruined in their ridiculous attempts to keep up appearances and make a 'sensation.'

"I know a gentleman of fortune who says that, when he first began to prosper, his wife thought she must have a new and elegant sofa. 'That sofa,' he said, 'cost me thirty thousand dollars.' When the sofa reached the house, it was found necessary to get chairs to match; then sideboards, carpets, and tables to 'correspond' with them, and so on through the entire stock of furniture; when at length it was found that the house itself was quite too small and old-fashioned for the furniture, and a new one was built to correspond with the new purchases; 'thus,' added my friend, 'summing up an outlay of thirty thousand dollars caused by that single sofa, and saddling on me in the shape of servants, equipage, and the necessary expenses attendant upon keeping up a fine "establishment," a yearly outlay of eleven thousand dollars, and a tight pinch at that; whereas, ten years before, we lived with much more real comfort, because with much less care, on as many hundreds. The truth is that that sofa would have brought me to inevitable bankruptcy, had not a most unexampled tide of prosperity kept me above it, and had I not checked the natural desire to "cut a dash."'"

In order to prosper, you must learn, must *realize*, must FEEL, the value of money. Never forget that, when honestly made, the money which comes to you in the pursuit of your legitimate vocation, is, or ought to be, as a shrewd writer has observed, the measure of your worth to the community you serve.

IN FINANCE, AS IN PHYSICS, ACTION AND REACTION ARE EQUAL.

"I have discovered that there is money enough in the world for all of us, if it was only equally divided," said a spendthrift to a wealthy friend; "this should be done, and we would all be happy together."

"But if everybody was like you," said the rich man, "it would all be spent in two months. What would you do then?"

"Oh! divide again; keep dividing, of course."

Theoretically some such arrangement as this might afford a very easy and agreeable settlement of all our financial difficulties; but in actual practice, in this hard-headed, workday world, those who have the money are unanimously and uncompromisingly opposed to the plan, and will give us gold or silver willingly only in compensation for services rendered, and will demand it back again in exact proportion to the services we compel them or even permit them to render to us.

"I am not pausing to discuss here," says Florence Bell, "the desirability that the affluent should employ part of their means in a way which appears to most people so obviously 'right,' according to the received doctrines of altruism, that it is needless to spend time in discussing it. I am not going to repeat a thought that occurs in so many wise and foolish forms to most human minds, at either end of the social scale, that part of the means of the rich should be consecrated to helping those who deserve help, or even those who simply need it. In both cases I would say incidentally that it is always possible to find out whether they do either the one or the other, though this means a great deal more trouble than enunciating a general reluctance to 'pauperize.' It may sometimes be allowable to act for the legitimate advantage of the individual on lines which would not be practicable if applied to the community. But the welfare of the two appear, at first sight, so inextricably interwined that it is no doubt more easy to say that the one must not be attempted for fear of endangering the other, than carefully and patiently to disentangle, for a given contingency, the threads that bind them together.

"As for the really, absolutely poor, those in whom every generous impulse, every offer of help, every contribution toward the needs of another means, as the French say, paying with their person, depriving themselves of what they have to give to some one else, sitting up themselves at night by a neighbor's sick bed and thus practically taking their share of another's trouble, — I would almost go so far as to say that such an attitude of mind engenders certain high virtues which are practically unknown among those who, under similar circumstances, simply draw out their purses, or write letters, — and send somebody else. It is probably unavoidable. These acts of daily heroism and self-sacrifice, accomplished as a matter of course at the cost of personal fatigue, suffering, and privation, are things that cannot be learned in theory, and are likely to be practiced but very exceptionally by those who can exercise them by proxy. Is it true, then, after all, — can it be? — that there is a high level of moral achievement which it may be difficult for the rich to attain? — certain qualities, and those of the finest kind, which are bound to lie dormant, if circumstances do not call them forth? If so, let us seek for the remedy in the right place. Thrift is not the virtue we need here. It is not so simple as that. What is needed is to make a vigorous stand against the action of surroundings and circumstances, lest we should fall a helpless prey to them; to keep alive by constant effort the conviction that it is necessary to resist them. But it is possible that those whose lives are sunny and prosperous may mistake the content and satisfaction they feel for a condition of moral excellence in which watchfulness is not so much needed. Plato tells us that it is difficult to be cheerful when you are old and poor; and we may presume, therefore, that it is not difficult when you are old and rich. But even granting that that is so, which it certainly is not invariably, — for otherwise we should have a whole class of cheerful old rich whose existence would be of the greatest gain to the community, — that is not the highest form of excellence. That is the sort of wellbeing that comes from repletion; you have had your fill of the good things of life, and can sit down well content. It is not philosophical and spiritual calm, arrived at by effort and aspiration. The obvious and disheartening condition of the people who have had enough is that they do not want more, and therefore do not try to attain it. This it is that may stop the strenuous impulse, both of a moral and mental kind; for the intelligence, as well as the character, may mistake the satisfactory development arrived at by helpful circumstance, for natural endowment. But still this condition, this kind of 'goodness,' which is what, on the whole, the most favorably situated average human being may hope to attain, is of the kind which is the second best. For, after admitting the value of money in procuring the possession, or even in eking out the perception, of the really good things in this world, we must recognize that these are still but joys of the second order. The chosen know something else. There are, happily, some left in the world who, having but little means, do not care about having more, all their desires and their possibilities being divinely absorbed in the possession of some great and glorious gift, — or even, failing the gift, the contemplation and pursuit of some lofty ideal."

SAY "NO!" AT NEED, AND SAVE FOR YOUR NEED.

"Another great point is to be able to say 'No,' on proper occasions," says Samuel Smiles. "When enticements allure, or temptations assail, say 'No' at once, resolutely and determinedly, — 'No; I can't afford it.' Many have not the moral courage to adopt this course. They consider only their selfish gratification. They are unable to practice self-denial. They yield, give way, and 'enjoy themselves.' The end is often defalcation, fraud, and ruin. What is the verdict of society in such cases? 'The man has been living beyond his means.' Of those who may have been entertained by him, not one of them will thank him, not one of them will pity him, not one of them will help him.

"Every one has heard of the man who could n't say 'No.' He was everybody's friend but his own. His worst enemy was himself. He ran rapidly through his means, and then called upon his friends for bonds, bails, and 'promises to pay.' After spending his last guinea, he died in the odor of harmless stupidity and folly.

"His course in life seemed to be directed by the maxim of doing for everybody what everybody asked him to do. Whether it was that his heart beat responsive to every other heart, or that he did not like to give offense, could never be ascertained; but certain it is that he was rarely asked to sign a requisition, to promise a vote, to lend money, or to indorse a bill, that he did not comply. He could n't say 'No;' and there were many, who knew him well, who said he had not the moral courage to do so.

"His father left him a snug little fortune, and he was at once beset by persons wanting a share of it. Then was the time to say 'No,' if he could, but he could n't. His habit of yielding had been formed; he did not like to be bored; could not bear to refuse; could not withstand importunity; and almost invariably yielded to the demands made upon his purse. While his money lasted, he had no end of friends. He was a universal referee, — everybody's bondsman. 'Just sign me this little bit of paper,' was a request often made to him by particular friends. 'What is it?' he would mildly ask; for, with all his simplicity, he prided himself upon his caution! Yet he never refused. Three months afterwards, a bill for a rather heavy amount would fall due, and who should be called upon to make it good but everybody's friend — the man who could n't say 'No.'"

Learn early in life to say "I can't afford it." It is an indication of power and courage and manliness. Dr. Franklin said, "It is not our own eyes, but other people's, that ruin us." "Fashion wears out more apparel than the man," says Shakespeare.

"That we are born 'free and equal' is a glorious truth, in one sense," says P. T. Barnum; "yet we are not all born equally rich, and we never shall be. One may say: 'There is a man who has an income of fifty thousand dollars per annum, while I have but one thousand dollars; I knew that fellow when he was poor like myself: now he is rich and thinks he is better than I am; I will show him that I am as good as he is; I will go and buy a horse and buggy; — no, I cannot do that, but I will go and hire one and ride this afternoon on the same road that he does, and thus prove to him that I am as good as he is.'

"My friend, you need not take that trouble, for you can easily prove that you are 'as good as he is;' you have only to behave as well as he does, but you cannot make anybody believe that you are as rich as he is. Besides, if you put on those 'airs,' and waste your time and spend your money, your poor wife will be obliged to scrub her fingers off at home, and buy her tea two ounces at a time, and everything else in proportion, in order that you may keep up 'appearances,' and, after all, deceive nobody. On the other hand, Mrs. Smith may say that her next-door neighbor married Johnson for his money, and 'everybody says so.' The latter has a nice thousand-dollar camel's-hair shawl, and so Mrs. Smith will make Smith get her an imitation one, and she will sit in a pew right next to her neighbor in church, in order to prove that she is her equal.

"My good woman, you will not get ahead in the world if your vanity and envy thus take the lead. In this country, where we believe the majority ought to rule, we ignore that principle in regard to fashion, and let a handful of people, calling themselves the aristocracy, run up a false standard of perfection; and, in endeavoring to rise to that standard, we constantly keep ourselves poor, all the time digging away for the sake of outside appearances. How much wiser it would be to be a 'law unto ourselves,' and say, ' We will regulate our outgo by our income, and lay up something for a rainy day.' People ought to be as sensible on the subject of money-getting as on any other subject. Like causes produce like effects. You cannot accumulate a fortune by taking the road that leads to poverty. It needs no prophet to tell us that those who live fully up to their means, without any thought of a reverse in this life, can never attain pecuniary independence."

"A great many young men make their way to the city annually," said a Wall Street financier quoted by W. J. Tilley, " deserting the farm, the country store, and light occupations in small towns, ambitious to wrestle for the spoils of commerce and the golden fruits of trade, without the slightest knowledge of how to live on small pay.

" The first lesson I had to learn was how to spend my money, — how to make a small salary put food into my mouth, clothes on my back, and a roof over me. Strange as it may seem, some never learn the lesson, and go disgraced through debt, broken through disappointment, and useless, by reason of their city experience. A boy coming to this city with a few dollars must learn how to get what he wants at the least possible cost. He must be shown how to do this. This knowledge will be more beneficial to him than a place. He must know that every penny saved is a penny made. Look at our rich men. Many of them slept under the counters in the stores, and had only bread and milk for breakfast. Read the stories of A. T. Stewart, Edwin D. Morgan, John Jacob Astor, Pierre Lorillard, Isaac T. Sherman, Jay Gould, and Cornelius Vanderbilt. Why, those men matched their stomachs and their backs to the pennies in their pockets, and the pennies won, for they saved them."

"What can a cent do?" asked a missionary. "It can accomplish very little by itself. It can buy a pretzel or a stick of candy, which has a mysterious faculty of melting away before one has had time to enjoy having it. It can lose itself out of the smallest hole in its owner's pocket; it cannot buy a loaf of bread, or pay a car-fare, or do anything else that is useful or interesting. The consequence is that it is perfectly wonderful how many pennies even very poor children have.

"But, though it is not good for much in itself, the penny is an excellent help in a sum in addition. If a boy's mother, every time he asks her for a penny, were to put it into a little box instead of giving it to him, and he were to add them all up at the end of the year, how many do you suppose there would be? Ask her to try it, and see. And as for multiplying, you would never dream what the penny can do with the multiplication table. True, it is a dull, insignificant copper thing; but multiply it by a hundred, and you can get a nice, crisp, new dollar bill with the result.

"Ten little round cents from each of two hundred thousand boys and girls, little and big, — what can they do, do you think? They can pay the salaries and traveling expenses of a dozen or more Sunday-school missionaries, and give them some thousands of dollars to help them carry on their work. They can help to start a dozen new churches."

Aggregated pennies constitute the capital which employs armies of laborers and makes the wheels of progress go round. Nearly every great fortune of our day represents the vast sum total of a multiplicity of small profits. *But the little profits must be added, or there will be no great result, — no powerful fund of savings.*

"OUT OF DEBT, — OUT OF DANGER!"

"Half the battle of existence depends upon the ability of a young economist to control his expenses in accordance with his means."

> He that a vice from year to year inherits
> Wieldeth an ax against his tree of merits.
> *Oriental Poetry.*

All fortunes have their foundations laid in economy. — *J. G. Holland.*

Debt is, like any other trap, easy enough to get into, but hard enough to get out of. — *H. W. Shaw.*

A large part of every man's time must needs be consumed, in one sense, for the sake of giving potency to the residue. It is remarkable how the principle of the use and waste of one thing for another pervades creation. One third of our time is thrown into sleep. It dies, that the other two thirds may live to be of worth. For every two hours of living, full of strength, there has been one sacrificed hour that laid itself down for them. — *H. W. Beecher.*

"Mr. Speaker," exclaimed the eccentric John Randolph, of Roanoke, in a piercing voice, as he sprang from his seat in the United States House of Representatives; "Mr. Speaker, I have found it!" Then, in the stillness which followed this strange outburst, he added: "I have found the Philosopher's Stone: it is *Pay as you go.*"

"But suppose I can't pay!" suggested a young man whose uncle had just told him this story, emphasizing its moral.

"Then don't go," replied the uncle.

"What! so early at your desk!" exclaimed Napoleon, on the way to his bath, as he heard some one humming a tune and found that it was one of his secretaries. The great commander had already been at work for some time. "Why," he continued, "this is very exemplary. We ought to be well satisfied with such service. What salary have you?"

"Twelve hundred dollars, sire," was the reply.

"Indeed," said Napoleon, "that, for one of your age, is very handsome. In addition, I think, you have your board and lodging."

"I have, sire."

"Well, I do not wonder that you sing. You must be a very happy man."

"Alas, sire, I ought to be, but I am not."

"And why not?"

"Because I have too many *English* tormenting me. I have, also, an aged father, who is almost blind, and a sister who is not yet married, dependent upon me for support."

"But, sir," said Napoleon, "in supporting your father and your sister, you do only that which every good son would do. But what have you to do with the *English?*"

"They are those," replied the secretary, "who have loaned me money, which I am not able to repay. All Frenchmen who are in debt call their creditors the *English.*"

This was the real explanation of the young man's eagerness to work. He had passed a sleepless night, thinking of his debts, and had risen early to find distraction from his thoughts. For a similar reason he sought refuge from his cares in singing.

"Enough! enough!" said Napoleon, "I understand you. You are in debt. And how is it that, with such a salary, you run into debt? I wish to have no man about my person who has recourse to the gold of the *English*. From this hour you will receive your dismission. Adieu, sir." Saying this, he left the young man stupefied with despair. But a few moments later an aid entered and handed him a note, saying, "It is from Napoleon." It read: —

"I have wished to dismiss you from my cabinet, for you deserve it; but I have thought of your aged and blind father, and of your young sister, and, for their sake, I pardon you. Further, since they are the ones who must most suffer from your misconduct, I send you, with leave of absence for one day only, the sum of two thousand dollars. With this sum disembarrass yourself immediately of all the *English* who trouble you, and hereafter conduct yourself in such a manner as not to fall into their power. Should you fail in this, I shall give you leave of absence without permission to return."

"If you want to test a young man and ascertain whether nature made him for a king or a subject," says James Parton, "give him a thousand dollars and see what he will do with it. If he is born to conquer and command, he will put it quietly away till he is ready to use it as opportunity offers. If he is born to serve, he will immediately begin to spend it in gratifying his ruling propensity."

"On the first rule of the art of managing money," says Bulwer, "all preceptors must be agreed. It is told in three words, — 'horror of debt.'

"Nurse, cherish, never cavil away the wholesome horror of debt. Personal liberty is the paramount essential to human dignity and human happiness. Debt is to man what the serpent is to the bird; its eye fascinates, its breath poisons, its coil crushes sinew and bone, its jaw is the pitiless grave. If you mock my illustration, if you sneer at the truth it embodies, give yourself no further trouble to learn how to manage your money. Consider yourself doomed; pass on your way with a jaunty step; the path is facile,— paths to Avernus always are. But if, while I write, your heart, true to the instinct of manhood, responds to my words,— if you say, 'agreed; that which you call the first rule for the management of money, I hold yet more imperative as the necessity to freedom and the lifespring of probity,' — then advance on your way, assured that, wherever it may wind, it must ascend. You see but the temple of Honor; close behind it is the temple of Fortune. You will pass through the one to the other.

"Three years ago you admired the rising success of some most respectable man. Where is he now? In the dock,— in the jail,— in the hulks! What! that opulent banker, whose plate dazzled princes? — or that flourishing clerk, who drove the high-stepping horse to his office? The same. And his crime? Fraud and swindling. What demon could urge so respectable a man to so shameful an act? I know not the name of the demon, but the cause of the crime the wretch tells you himself. Ask him; what is his answer? 'I got into debt; there was no way out of it but the one which I took,— to the dock, to the jail, to the hulks.'

"Easy to keep out of debt? No, my young friend, it is difficult. Are you rich? The bland tradesman cries, 'Pay when you please!' Your rents or your father's allowance will not be due for three months; your purse, in the meanwhile, cannot afford you some pleasant vice or some innocent luxury which to some may seem a want. You are about to relinquish the vice or dispense with the

JOHN RANDOLPH, OF ROANOKE,
For thirty years a member of the House of Representatives.

b. 1773; d. 1833.

luxury, when a charming acquaintance, who lives no one knows how, though no one lives better, introduces an amiable creature, sleek as a cat, with paws of velvet hiding claws of steel; his manners are pleasing, his calling is — usury. You want the money for three months. Why say *three?* Your name to the bill for six months will make the vice or the luxury yours the next hour. Certainly, the easy thing here is to put your name to the bill. But, presto! you are in debt; the demon has you down in his books!

"Now comes the next danger. You will not incur debt for yourself, but you have a friend. Pythias, your friend, your familiar, the man you like best and see most of, says to you: 'Damon, be my security; put your name to this bill!'

"Can you pay the money if Pythias does not? If you cannot pay, or if you owe it to others more sacred than Pythias himself — owe it to your parents, your plighted bride, or wedded wife, or the children to whom what, before their birth, was your fortune, has become the trust money for their provision, — not to hazard for Pythias that for which, if lost, not you alone but others must suffer, then do not common duty and common honesty forbid you to become surety to Pythias for an obligation which belongs not to Pythias, but to chance, to repay?

"'My name!' falters Damon; 'I am but a surety. Go to Pythias.'

"'Pythias has bolted!'

"Pay the bill, Damon, or good-by to your honor!

"Pardon my prolixity; earnestness is apt to be garrulous. *Vixi!* I have lived and known life. Alas, what careers bright in promise I have seen close in jail or exile; what talents, profuse in their blossom, die off without coming to fruit; what virtues the manliest rot into vices the meanest, which, when one cried, in amazement, 'How can you account for so doleful an end to so fair a commencement?' solve their whole mystery in this: 'Damon never recovered from his first fatal error; he put his name to a bill by which Pythias promised to pay so and so in three months.'

"Having settled these important preliminaries, — first, never to borrow when there is a chance, however remote, that you may not be able to pay; second, never to lend what you are not prepared to give; third, never to guarantee for another what you cannot fulfill if the other should fail, — you start in life with the great advantage that whatever you have, be it little or much, is your own. Rich or poor, you start as a freeman, resolved to preserve in your freedom the noblest condition of your being a man."

He who is a spendthrift is usually a borrower; and "Poor Richard" wisely declares, "He who goes a-borrowing goes a-sorrowing." Debt is one of man's worst tyrants.

"Be no man's debtor," says a good adviser. "I can give you no better motto to rule your life by, — whether as son to parent, employee to employer, husband to wife, father to child, debtor to creditor, or creditor to debtor, — resolve to be under obligations to no man, indebted to none. Thrift is the seed that must be sown before you can reap the subsequent harvest, that pecuniary independence essential to a life of virtue and happiness. There is no sacrifice too great to avoid the misery of debt. Think of what is due to yourself as a man, and do your duty manfully; resolve to be 'no man's debtor.'

Very well for you, some say; fortune has favored you; you have been one of the fortunate ones in this life. Only those who wear the shoes know where they pinch. Mine has been a hard up-hill fight from the first to the last; and, when comparing your life with that of others, it is as well to remember that, in every life, even in those which seem brightest and fairest, there is some grave where dead hopes and unfulfilled dreams lie buried."

"Avoid debt as you would the devil," was Beecher's advice to his son. Make up your mind never to have your name on any man's books, for personal expenses of any kind. This getting trusted for a box of collars, or a toothpick, is bad practice, besides being expensive. No dealer will take his chance of losing, without a round profit.

"Annual income," says Micawber, "twenty pounds; annual expenditure, nineteen six, result — happiness. Annual income, twenty pounds; annual expenditure, twenty pounds ought and six, result — misery."

"A man in debt is not his own master," says Smiles; "he is at the mercy of the tradesmen he employs. He is the butt of lawyers, the byword of creditors, the scandal of neighbors; he is a slave in his own house; his moral character becomes degraded and defiled; and even his own household and family regard him with pity akin to contempt."

"Young men starting in life should avoid running into debt," said P. T. Barnum. "There is scarcely anything else that drags a person down like it. It is a slavish condition to get into, yet we find many a man hardly out of his 'teens' running in debt. He meets a chum and says, 'Look at this: I have got trusted for a new suit of clothes.' He seems to look upon the clothes as so much given to him. Well, it frequently is so; but, if he succeeds in paying and then gets trusted again, he is adopting a habit which will keep him in poverty through life. Debt robs a man of his self-respect, and makes him almost despise himself. Grunting and groaning and working for what he has eaten up or worn out, and now when he is called upon to pay, he has nothing to show for his money; this is properly termed 'working for a dead horse.' I do not speak of merchants buying and selling on credit, or of those who buy on credit in order to turn a purchase to a profit. An old Friend said to his son, a farmer: 'John, never get trusted; but, if thee gets trusted for anything, let it be for fertilizers, because they will help thee pay the amount credited again.'

"Money is, in some respects, like fire, — it is a very excellent servant but a terrible master. When you have it mastering you, when interest is constantly piling up against you, it will keep you down in the worst kind of slavery. But let money work for you, and you have the most devoted servant in the world. It is no 'eye-servant.' There is nothing else, animate or inanimate, that will work so faithfully as money when placed at interest, and well secured. It works night and day, and in wet or dry weather."

To do your best you must own every bit of yourself. If you are in debt, part of you belongs to your creditors. Nothing but actual sin is so paralyzing to a young man's energies as debt.

"Hunger, rags, cold, hard work, suspicion, and unjust reproach are disagreeable," said Horace Greeley; "but debt is infinitely worse than them all. If I had but fifty cents a week to live on, I'd buy a peck of corn and parch it before I'd owe any man a dollar."

"Of what a hideous progeny of ill is debt the father," said Douglas W. Jerrold. "What meanness, what invasions of self-respect, what cares, what double-dealing! How in due season it will carve the frank, open face into wrinkles; how like a knife it will stab the honest heart. And then its transformations, — how it has been known to change a goodly face into a mask of brass; how with this evil custom of debt has the true man become a callous trickster! A freedom from debt, and what nourishing sweetness may be found in cold water; what toothsomeness in a dry crust; what ambrosial nourishment in a hard egg! Be sure of it, he who dines out of debt, though his meal be a biscuit and an onion, dines in 'The Apollo.' And then for raiment, what warmth in a threadbare coat, if the tailor's receipt be in your pocket! What Tyrian purple in the faded waistcoat, the vest not owed for; how glossy the well-worn hat, if it covers not the aching head of a debtor! Next, think of the home sweets, the outdoor recreation of the free man. The street door falls not a knell in his heart; the foot on the staircase, though he lives on the third pair, sends no spasm through his anatomy; at the rap on his door he can crow 'Come in,' and his pulse still beats healthfully. See him abroad! How he returns look for look with any passenger. Poverty is a bitter draught, yet may, and sometimes can with advantage, be gulped down. Though the drinker makes wry faces, there may, after all, be a wholesome goodness in the cup. But debt, however courteously it may be offered, is the Cup of Siren; and the wine, spiced and delicious though it be, is poison. My son, if poor, see Hyson in the running spring; see thy mouth water at last week's roll; think a threadbare coat the only wear; and acknowledge a whitewashed garret the fittest housing-place for a gentleman; do this, and flee debt. So shall thy heart be at rest, and the sheriff confounded."

It has become a part of the new political economy to argue that a debt on a church or a house or a farm is a desirable thing to develop character. When a young man starts out in life with the old-fashioned idea strong in his mind that debt is bondage and a disgrace, that a mortgage is to be shunned like the cholera, and that to owe a dollar that you cannot pay, unless overtaken by misfortune, is nothing more or less than stealing, then he is bound, in so much at least, to succeed, and save his old age from being a burden upon his friends or the state.

"Owe no man anything," says St. Paul.

TO PROSPER ONE MUST BE "ALL THERE."

"To make money requires a clear brain," said P. T. Barnum; "a man must see that two and two make four; he must lay all his plans with reflection and forethought, and closely examine all the details, and the ins and outs of business. As no man can succeed in business unless he has a brain to enable him to lay his plans, and reason to guide him in their execution, so, no matter how bountifully one may be blessed with intelligence, if his brain is muddled, and his judgment warped by intoxicating drinks, it is impossible for him to carry on business successfully. How many good opportunities have passed, never to return, while a man was taking 'a social glass' with a friend! How many foolish bargains have been made under the influence of wine, which temporarily makes its victim think he is rich! How many important chances have been put off until to-morrow, and then forever, because the wine cup has thrown the system into a state of lassitude, neutralizing the energies so essential to success in business! Verily, 'wine is a mocker.' The use of intoxicating drinks as a beverage is as much an infatuation as is the smoking of opium by the Chinese, and the former is quite as destructive to the success of the business man as is the latter. It is an unmitigated evil, utterly indefensible in the light of philosophy, religion, or good sense. It is the parent of nearly every other evil in our country."

A New Orleans printer, when his fellow-workmen went out to drink beer during working hours, put in the bank the exact amount which he would have spent if he had gone with them. He pursued this plan for five years, when he examined his bank account and found he had deposited five hundred and twenty-one dollars and eighty-six cents. In the five years he had not lost a day on account of sickness. Three out of five of the others had in the meantime become drunkards, were worthless as workmen, and were discharged. The water drinker then bought the printing office, enlarged the business, and, twenty years from the time he began to put by his money, was worth one hundred thousand dollars.

"It may seem strange," says the "Sanitarian," "but it is nevertheless true, that alcohol regularly applied to a thrifty farmer's stomach will remove the boards from his fences, let cattle into his crops, kill his fruit trees, mortgage his farm, and sow his fields with wild oats and thistles; may take the paint off his buildings, break the glass in his windows, and fill them with rags. It will take the poor, see Hyson clothes and polish from his

Sorry:
The defect on the previous page was that way in the original book we reproduced.

manners, subdue his reason, arouse his passions, bring sorrow and disgrace upon his family, and topple him into a drunkard's grave. It will do this to the artisan and the capitalist, the matron and the maiden, as well as to the farmer, for in its deadly enmity to the human race alcohol is no respecter of persons."

When fondness for dissipation takes possession of a mind which does not realize the constituent elements of a dollar, it will sweep through a fortune like fire through prairie-grass, gaining force and momentum from what it destroys. The daily papers recently gave the story of a spendthrift who had squandered a legacy of $160,000 from his grandmother, and one of $435,000 from an uncle; and, although his mother had left him a trust fund of $300,000, yielding an income of $12,000 a year, he had borrowed heavily from a brother and a sister, raised all he could on his wife's property, and then failed with liabilities of $29,000 and assets of $4,600. All this he accomplished in about three years!

A NICKEL A DAY BOUGHT HIS LIBRARY.

"What do you do with all those books?" asked a young man of a friend whom he found reading, with more than a hundred volumes around him.

"Oh, that library is my one cigar a day," was the response.

"What do you mean?"

"I mean just this: when you bothered me so about being a man and advising me to learn to smoke, I'd recently been reading about a young fellow who bought books with money that others would have spent in smoke, and I thought I'd try to do the same. You will remember that I said I should allow myself one cigar a day."

"Yes, I do."

"Well, I did not smoke, but put by the price of a five-cent cigar every day, and, as the money accumulated, I bought books,—these you see here."

"Do you mean to say that these books cost no more than that? Why, I should think they were worth a hundred dollars!"

"Yes, I know there are a good many. I had six years more of apprenticeship when you tried to persuade me to be a man; I put by the money I have told you of, which, of course, at five cents a day, amounted to eighteen dollars and a quarter a year, or one hundred and nine dollars and a half in six years. I keep those books by themselves, as a result of my apprenticeship cigar-money; and, if you had done as I have, you would by this time have saved many, many more dollars than that, and been in business besides."

How true is the saying, "What maintains one vice would bring up two children!"

"But," said a "temperate" devotee of the weed, "I did not begin to smoke until I was twenty, and have never used more than eight cigars per week or paid more than ten cents apiece for them."

"That certainly seems moderate," said a friend; "but, if you should save the eighty cents per week and invest it every six months at seven per cent. compound interest, how much do you suppose it would amount to by your sixtieth birthday?"

The smoker was quick at figures, and soon replied: "Eight thousand, three hundred and eleven dollars."

"Very good!" said his friend; "now put *that* in your pipe and smoke it."

"Ten cents a day even," says an American writer, "is

thirty-six dollars and a half a year, and that is the interest on a capital of six hundred dollars; so that the man who saves ten cents a day only is as much richer than he who does not as if he owned a life estate in a property worth six hundred dollars."

Great, however, as are the money-cost and the health-cost of smoking, the sacrifice of freedom or independence is even greater. Many a youth who smokes cigarettes cannot truthfully say that his soul is his own. A victim stated recently that he had often walked four miles to town to save car-fare in order that he might buy a package of cigarettes.

SUCCESSFUL FINANCIERS KEEP CAREFUL ACCOUNTS.

Waste neither time nor money, but make the best use of both.
Franklin.

"A habit of keeping a strict account of personal expenses down to the pennies has great educational power."

He that thinks he can afford to be negligent is not far from being poor. — *Johnson.*

> Yet was she not profuse, but feared to waste,
> And wisely managed that the stock might last;
> That all might be supplied, and she not grieve,
> When crowds appeared, she had not to relieve;
> Which to prevent, she still increased her store,
> Laid up, and spared, that she might give the more.
> *Dryden.*

"I have often been asked to define the true secret of success," says Sir Thomas J. Lipton. "It is thrift in all its phases, and principally thrift as applied to saving. A young man may have many friends, but he will find none so steadfast, so constant, so ready to respond to his wants, so capable of pushing him ahead as a little leather-covered book, with the name of a bank on its cover. Saving is the first great principle of all success. It creates independence, it gives a young man standing, it fills him with vigor, it stimulates him with the proper energy; in fact, it brings to him the best part of any success, — happiness and contentment. If it were possible to inject the quality of saving into every boy, we should have a great many more real men."

"A knowledge of arithmetic is absolutely necessary to those who would live within their means," says Smiles. "Women are especially ignorant of arithmetic; they are scarcely taught the simplest elements, for female teachers think the information useless. They prefer to teach languages, music, deportment, and the use of globes. All these may be important, but the first four rules of arithmetic are better than all else. How can they compare their expenditures with their receipts, without the knowledge of addition and subtraction? How can they know precisely what to spend in rent, or clothing, or food, or for service, unless they know the value of figures? How can they check the accounts of their tradesmen or their servants? This want of knowledge of arithmetic is the cause, not only of great waste, but also of great misery. Many a family of good position has fallen into destitution merely because of its ignorance of this branch of knowledge."

Washington examined the minutest expenditures of his family, even when President of the United States. He understood that without economy none can be rich, and with it none need be poor.

"I make a point of paying my own bills," said Wellington. He took account of all his expenditures. So did his great opponent.

"It is one of the miracles of Napoleon," says the historian Ingersoll, "that he waged all his enormous wars without contracting a debt or borrowing a cent, without discounting a note or using one not forthwith convertible into coin; and, when expelled from the throne, he left in the cellars of his palace a large sum — many millions in cash, — economized from family show for public service. The imperial budget of France, when he ruled fifty millions of subjects, was little more than half the royal budget when Louis Philippe ruled over thirty-four millions. The standard of probity was as much higher in Napoleon's time. . . . Although it may be said that he supported France by the conquests which England, by successive coalitions, forced him to make, yet the abundance, regularity, and management of the national income and expenditures in his time, without an idea of what is now recognized as the science of political economy, without paper money and without debt, is a monument as amazing as his code of laws."

All or nearly all great generals have been careful calculators. Even while striking those sledge-hammer blows upon Lee's army in the Wilderness, — fighting it out on that line, if it should take all summer, with many newspapers in the North calling him a "butcher" and clamoring for his recall, — Grant was considering and providing for the end as well as the beginning of the great movement. When at length his troops crossed the James River, they found waiting for them thousands of barrels of provisions which their commander had ordered Gen. B. F. Butler to transport thither by way of City Point and Bermuda Hundred. So, in individual life, each person is the general of his own personal forces, and should manage his treasury and commissary departments with the wisdom of a leader, if he would win life's battles.

English working men and women work very hard, seldom take a holiday, and, though they get nearly double the wages of the same classes in France, yet save very little. The millions earned by them slip out of their hands almost as soon as obtained, to satisfy the pleasures of the moment. In France every housekeeper is taught the art of making much out of little. "I am simply astonished," writes an American lady stopping in France, "at the number of good wholesome dishes which my friend here makes for her table from things which, at home, I always throw away, — dainty little dishes from scraps of cold meat, from hard crusts of bread, delicately prepared and seasoned, from almost everything and nothing. And yet there is no feeling of stinginess or want."

"Where there is no prudence," says Dr. Johnson, "there is no virtue."

"So apportion your wants that your means may exceed them," says Bulwer. "With one hundred pounds a year I may need no man's help; I may at least have 'my crust of bread and liberty.' But with five thousand pounds a year, I may dread a ring at my bell; I may have my tyrannical master in servants whose wages I cannot pay; my exile may be at the fiat of the first long-suffering man who enters a judgment against me; for the flesh that lies nearest my heart, some Shylock may be dusting his scales and whetting his knife. Every man is needy who spends more than he has; no man is needy who spends less. I may so ill manage that, with five thousand pounds a year, I purchase the worst evils of poverty, — terror and shame; I may so well manage my money that, with one hundred pounds a year, I purchase the best blessings of wealth, — safety and respect."

THE CASH VALUE OF EDUCATION.

Ignorance is the mortal enemy of thrift. A thoroughly educated mind is usually a creator of values, material, mental, and spiritual.

"Any man is educated," says Minot J. Savage, "who is so developed and trained that, drop him where you will in the world, he is able to master his circumstances and deal with the facts of life so as to build up in himself a noble manhood and be of service to those about him. That is what education means; that is what it is for. Knowledge of foreign tongues, a list of historic facts concerning the past, information poured into a man's brain, — these things are not education. There are learned fools."

School Commissioner N. C. Schaeffer, of Pennsylvania, thus shows the actual cash value of an education: —

"An Indiana jury awarded $599.99 for the killing of a boy. A friend of mine, who is a superintendent in West Virginia, called that award an outrage. I asked him why? He answered, 'To say nothing of the boy's personality and all that a boy is to his father and mother and home, the commercial value of a boy's time at school is more than the award of that Indiana jury.' I asked him how he made the calculation. He said, 'You find the value of a boy's time at school by subtracting the earnings of a life of uneducated labor from the earnings of a life of educated labor.' Then he gave me a calculation that

I have used before institutes, for I am anxious to get it into the daily papers, to have it carried to every schoolroom and put upon every blackboard, so that the pupils may carry it home and discuss it with their parents.

"He said: 'If an uneducated man earns one dollar and fifty cents a day for three hundred days in the year, he does very well, and if he keeps it up for forty years he will earn $1.50 × 300 × 40, or $18,000. An educated man is not generally paid by the day, but by the month and by the year. If you will strike an average of the earnings of educated men, beginning with the President of the United States, who earns $50,000 a year, the presidents of insurance companies and of the large railroad companies, and run down the scale, until you come to the lower walks in point of earnings among educated men, you will admit that $1,000 a year is a low average for the earnings of educated labor. For forty years you have $40,000 as the earnings of an educated man. Subtract $18,000 from $40,000, and the difference, or $22,000, must represent the value of a boy's time spent at school in getting an education.' You will admit that the man who works with his hands at unskilled labor puts forth as much muscular effort as the man who earns his livelihood by his wits and education. Now, if $22,000 represents the value of the time that a boy spends at school in getting an education, what is the value of a day spent at school? The average school life of every boy and girl in Massachusetts is seven years of two hundred days each; let us say that it takes four years more to get a good education. Reckoning eleven years of two hundred days each, you will find that the 2,200 days at school are equal to $22,000, and a simple division on the blackboard will bring it home to the comprehension of every boy that every day at school, properly spent, must be worth ten dollars.

"What sort of letters do we get at the school department? One director asks whether it is a violation of the compulsory law if a farmer keeps at home his eleven-year-old boy to plow, because it costs one dollar a day to get some man to do the work. While he is putting one dollar into his own pocket, he is robbing that boy of ten dollars in the shape of future earning capacity. Is not that high-handed robbery by a father of his own child?

"In the legislature recently, the minimum term was lengthened from six to seven months; in other words, twenty days a year were added to the school life of 200,000 children. If time at school properly spent is worth ten dollars a day, then that act of the legislature should add to the future productiveness of the commonwealth ten dollars multiplied by twenty and that product by 200,000, or $40,000,000."

WAR IS WASTE; LITIGATION, EXPENSIVE.

Individual contentions at law and national contentions in war are among the greatest wasters of individual and national wealth. Sometimes they cannot well be avoided; but, whenever they can be with honor, they should be.

"I agree with you perfectly in your disapprobation of war," said Franklin. "I think it wrong in point of human prudence; for, whatever advantage one nation would obtain from another, it would be much cheaper to purchase such advantage with ready money, than to pay the expense of acquiring it by war. It seems to me that, if statesmen had a little more arithmetic, or were more accustomed to calculations, wars would be much less frequent."

JAMES A. GARFIELD,
Twentieth President of the United States.

b. 1831; d. 1881.

ECONOMY. 47

"Battles are never the end of war," said James A. Garfield, "for the dead must be buried, and the cost of the war must be paid, including pensions. One-tenth of our national debt, expended in public education fifty years ago, would have saved us the blood and treasure of the Civil War. School-houses are far less expensive than rebellions."

"Europe, from the North Cape to the Mediterranean," says John S. C. Abbott, "would be almost a garden of Eden, had the uncounted millions which have been expended in the desolation of war been appropriated to enriching and embellishing her sunny valleys and her romantic hillsides."

EQUANIMITY TENDS TO HEALTH AND WEALTH.

One of the greatest wastes of life is the result of loss of equanimity, as shown in anger, fretfulness, and profanity. Such things will be found, on reflection, to be wholly unnecessary.

"But are there examples in everyday life, among everyday people, that prove the possibility of superiority over anger and worry?" asks Horace Fletcher.

"Yes," he replies; "habitually profane men do not swear in the presence of ladies. Vicious men are gentle when among those whom they respect. The passions are subservient to the will under conditions that reverence or fashion prescribes. If they are subservient under any conditions, they can be controlled under all conditions. Nothing, for instance, could make you angry while we are talking on this subject, because you would feel ashamed to show slavery to a condemned and unmanly weakness."

"Once, when I was returning from Ireland," says

Rowland Hill, "I found myself much annoyed by the reprobate conduct of the mate and the captain, who were both given to the scandalous habit of swearing. First the captain swore at the mate, then the mate swore at the captain, then they both swore at the wind, when I called to them with a strong voice for fair play.

" ' Stop ! stop !' said I; 'if you please, gentlemen, let us have fair play; it is my turn now.'

" ' At what is it your turn, pray ? ' said the captain.

" ' At swearing,' I replied.

" Well, they waited and waited until their patience was exhausted, and then wanted me to make haste and take my turn. I told them, however, that I had a right to take my own time, and swear at my own convenience.

" To this the captain replied, with a laugh : —

" ' Perhaps you don't mean to take your turn ? '

" ' Pardon me, captain,' I answered, ' but I do, as soon as I can find the good of doing so.'

" My friends, I did not hear another oath on the voyage." Economy of this kind is generally easy and always profitable.

Cheerfulness and hopefulness are true economists; their opposites are among the greatest of spendthrifts. The former conserve all our powers and hearten them for the necessary struggles of life. The latter squander our strength in unnecessary doubt and discouragement. The force we waste upon our fears, it has been well said, is all that would be needed for the achievement of our purpose.

"The body is God's schoolmaster," says N. D. Hillis, "teaching industry, compelling economy and thrift, and promoting all the basal moralities. It contains the springs of all material civilization.

"Memory gathers up all our yesterdays. Often her writing is invisible, like that of a penman writing with lemon juice, taking note of each transgression and recording words that will appear when held up to the heat of fire."

How important it is, then, that the thoughts and emotions and resolves which build up our fund of character shall be such as to make that character really valuable! No bookkeeper takes visible note of these things; even the mind seldom keeps any account of them; and yet they accumulate in our savings bank of character with a usury beyond that of the money changers.

"Three hundred and sixty-five volumes in a year would be written," says Beecher, "if the definite reflections, motives, and emotions that every day pass distinctly through your mind, and have relation to your character and eternal destiny, should be printed in a book. What enormous fruitfulness! and how much of it seems to drop unnoticed! It is simply impossible for a man to take note of such a flow of inward life. One cannot keep pace even with that which is outward."

The Occident has taught the Orient many welcome and valuable lessons in civilization; let it take its pay by learning from Japan how to avoid anger and worry! So thoroughly has that country mastered what may be called the science of equanimity that even the babies, it is said, never cry in the fretful fashion of the Occident.

"You must first get rid of anger and worry," was the remark of a philosophic Japanese to a friend who was admiring the calm and quiet temper and temperament of the Oriental. "It is possible to the Japanese and ought to be to Americans."

"Brave, gentle, artistic, lovable little Japan," says

Horace Fletcher, "which, thirty odd years ago, was nursing in quiet seclusion a beautiful flower of artistic civilization, has been rudely but providentially forced into the community of nations to teach the rest of the world a great lesson in the art of true living."

"A mere wild, ungoverned, and ungovernable impulse of pain, directed to no good purpose whatsoever, submerging the mind and smothering the mental powers, is always bad," says Beecher. "There may be moments when sorrow is uncontrollable, and when one is relieved by giving way to it; there are bursts of sorrow which are but the experiences of the hour or the day, and it is better to let them spend themselves, and not narrowly mark their bounds and passages; but all sorrow, beyond the first relief of agonized feelings, should be held in check."

JUDICIOUS LIBERALITY PROMOTES PROSPERITY.

Avarice is more opposite to economy than is liberality.
La Rochefoucauld.

The minutes saved by hurry are as useless as the pennies saved by parsimony. — *C. B. Newcomb.*

Be thrifty, not covetous; therefore give thy need, thine honor, and thy friend his due. — *George Herbert.*

Economy does not mean stinginess. It is not merely the withholding of money, but even more its wise expenditure, that constitutes careful financial management.

"We have warped the word *economy* in our English language into a meaning which it has no business to bear," says Ruskin. "In our use of it, it constantly signifies merely saving or sparing. Economy no more means saving money than it means spending money. It means the administration of a house; its stewardship; spending or saving money, or time, or anything else, to the best possible advantage."

Travelers will sometimes spend hours hunting for a boarding house or hotel at which they can save a franc or two a day, and afterwards find that they have located in a very inconvenient place. After spending hundreds, perhaps thousands of dollars to visit Europe, they will hesitate to spend five dollars for souvenirs which would add greatly to their pleasure in recalling the trip. They will buy cheap photographs or other works of art, which will fade or become useless in a few years. They will patronize the cheapest restaurants, where the food is often unwholesome or improperly cooked, when true economy requires the maintenance of health at its highest point if one would get all the pleasure and profit possible from such a journey.

"But thair iz sertin kinds of ekonomy that don't pa," says Josh Billings, "and one of them iz that thair iz a grate menny pepul in the world who try to ekonomize by stratenin' pins."

Such people will run all over town, visiting a dozen stores, trying to save a few cents on some small article they may wish to buy, — walking for miles to save carfare. In other words, they waste dollars' worth of precious time to save a few pennies.

Others will buy shoes or clothing because the price is low, although they should know that the articles will not wear well or long. They are never well dressed, and often pay more, in the end, than would be necessary to purchase durable, desirable clothing.

The best investments are not always those that have a percentage of profit in sight. Liberality often pays good returns. From a cold commercial point of view, aside from the nobler promptings of the heart, liberality pays. There is a magnetism about whole-souled men that wins patronage. People seldom calculate whether they will go to this doctor, or support that candidate, or buy at this or that store, but they are silently and harmoniously drawn toward people and institutions that are broad and liberal. There is a grand and subtle affinity in liberality worth working for, — a tonic to effort, that gives a winning personality.

"If I were out of employment, with only a dollar in the world, (and, if I did n't have a dollar, I would go out and earn one)," said the head of a firm who has risen from an office boy to his present position, "I would spend it all in an hour. I would divide most of that dollar between a shave, a bath, and a shine. With the remainder, I would buy the best meal I could get. I might have to carry a hod for my next meal, but never would I miss the one opportunity to make myself presentable for a better position." This would be economy. It is economy to patronize a good play or lecture. It is economy, as well as a paying investment, to buy good literature. It prompts high resolves and noble endeavor. It is economy to cultivate a desire for the best of everything in music and art. A piano in the house is economy. It is the creator of peace and harmony, which are priceless. It is economy to take a week's travel occasionally and learn what the world is doing beyond the four walls in which you live.

"I really can't afford to be too economical," said a woman recently. "I have a good neighbor who believes that every penny saved is a penny earned, and she looks her disapproval at me because I don't make over my own dresses and do buy my cakes. She does all those things herself and saves the money, and she makes me feel wasteful. Last year I tried to emulate her example, and I used up at least fifty dollars' worth of wife, mother, and family comfort, in trying to save twelve dollars' worth of sewing. Besides, there's the dressmaker's or the cakemaker's view of it to be taken into account, — for I suppose the 'neighbor' side of the question ought to come in somewhere.

"It reminds me of the cooking recipes which the newspapers gravely publish. I read one only yesterday. It was called a nice way to use up bits of cold mutton, but required fried cucumbers, thin pieces of broiled ham, several hard boiled eggs, soup stock, Worcestershire sauce, and so many other things, and so much time to prepare the dish, that it would make very expensive mutton of it. The ordinary housekeeper could n't afford to save it at that price. There is a great deal of so-called economy that is too costly for poor people."

An examination of the attics, closets, bureaus, cupboards, trunks, and basements of many an American home would reveal strange evidences of the unfortunate habit of saving useless articles. It seems really painful for some people to throw anything away, no matter if it costs twice as much as it is worth in valuable time to save it. This is not intelligent saving, the only kind that pays. It is far from the author's intention to encourage extravagance or waste; but, on the other hand, he wishes to emphasize the fact that the saving of mere "trumpery," without aim or purpose, is not the highest economy. Learn to let go, at the proper time, as well as to hold on. Remember that a broad, liberal policy pays best in these days, for a parsimonious, narrow-minded, stingy man seldom if ever becomes great, or conducts large business affairs. Always bear in mind what true economy is.

A habit of buying what one does not need, simply because it is cheap, encourages extravagance. Such investments are usually little more judicious than that of the widow who bought an old door-plate with the word "Thompson" on it, because she thought it might prove useful some time, although she was not acquainted with any gentleman of that name.

There is, perhaps, no wider-spread belief than that economy and meanness are twin brothers, while the fact is that they are not even distantly related. Economy is putting by that which there is no good reason for spending and good reason for retaining; meanness is withholding that which there is need of spending and no sufficient cause for retaining. Many a man has been called "a good fellow" because he prodigally squandered his earnings while his debts remained unpaid, and he was constantly putting himself in a position in which, should sickness overtake him, or his employment cease, he must become a burden to some one. There is nothing "good" about such a course, nor any meanness in foregoing present luxuries and indulgences for oneself or others that future independence and self-respect may be secured.

Live between extravagance and meanness. Don't save money and starve your mind. "The very secret and essence of thrift consists in getting things into higher values. Spend upward, — that is, for the higher faculties. Spend for the mind rather than for the body, for culture rather than for amusement. Some young men are too stingy to buy the daily papers, and are very ignorant and narrow. There is that withholdeth more than is meet, but it tendeth to poverty." Don't squeeze out of your life and comfort and family what you save.

"I once knew a man whose wife had a desire to have her photograph taken," says Henry Clews. "It was partly through harmless and perfectly proper vanity, and partly through a desire to have her children remember her at her best that she wished it, — for she was then young and beautiful. But her hard-fisted husband put off the gratification of her most cherished wish until routine life had done its inevitable work, and she was no longer lovely to look upon. She suffered her disappointment in silence. She brooded over the matter to such an extent that a mole-hill was magnified into a mountain, and eventually led to the estrangement of husband and wife and the breaking up of the family. His plea was 'economy.'

"What a dreadful paradox!

"What would one think of the engineer of a great steamship who would allow his engines to become disabled through a so-called too economical application of lubricating oil?

"I once knew a man many times a millionaire who would, upon leaving his library for dinner, always go around and lower the gas at each jet. Yet he would not stoop down to pick up a coin, because stooping down, he said, made him dizzy, and he would not think of incapacitating himself for any amount of money. I used also to know another very rich man whom I occasionally chided in a humorous way for burning so much gas, — having his rooms so brilliantly illuminated, — but his answer invariably was: 'What is the cost of gas compared to the cost of eyesight?' This man was a thorough, scientific economist, and so was the last-named man. They understood what the grand old word 'thrift' really means.

"Some people have most ridiculous ideas on this subject. A man once defined economy, in my presence, as 'a happy medium between parsimony and extravagance.' What could be more absurd? Thrift, the true economy, is wholly the opposite of either, so how can it logically be a combination or an average of the two?

"As I said before, true thrift consists in getting all the good you can out of everything; there is no economy in the bad. It is expensive to the point of wicked extravagance to deny oneself useful books, no matter what they cost, nor how poor one is; for what poverty is there like mental poverty?

"It is economy to pay a good price for a good seat at an entertainment, because in a good seat one is surrounded by inoffensive people and has no disturbing element to divert his mind. Before going to see a new play by new people, one should read the criticisms of it in the papers. Many a dollar is saved in this way. A play may be good enough for its purposes, yet possess no element of interest or profit to you. A newspaper costs only one or two cents, but a seat in a theater costs a dollar and a half. The economy of witnessing a good play is obvious. One may, for a comparatively trifling sum, enjoy all the benefits of a production which has cost thousands of dollars in time and money. On the other hand, to attend a poor play is the worst kind of extravagance, as you not only lose money, but your time as well, not to mention the wear and tear of your patience. I have heard men misuse the word in speaking of the gratification or denial of abnormal appetites.

This would be amusing, if it were not melancholy. If we might apply it in this way, I would say, for instance, that, if a man can get but one drink of whiskey for two dollars, the limit of his capital, it would be much more economical for him than to get twenty drinks for the same sum. This will not require any explanation.

"One other thing must always be remembered: that money represents the efforts of men. If one has a million dollars, he can for a day control a force equal to a million men, and in some countries even more. Every dollar one saves gives him practically control of the services of one man for one day, or gives him the privilege of resting for one day. When you hire a man to work in your garden, you don't keep him any longer than just long enough to accomplish the task you have set him to do, and so you save a fraction of a day's pay. Then you may go and squander an amount equal to what you have saved. You are throwing away so much force. No man can stand alone. His unsupported force is not sufficient for the battle of life. He must have help, and it must be that kind of help which he can absolutely control. Now money is the only force one can so control, as it represents labor, is the result of labor, and commands labor; and you have all that right in your pocket ready to carry out your wishes.

"One must make a study of the value of commodities in life, if he would expect to exist without being defrauded of much money. I never pay fifty cents for an article worth only twenty-five.

"The mere saving of pennies regardless of the sacrifices we make to save them is not scientific or practical thrift. It is not economy to pay a valuable man a small salary. There is too much of the 'saving at the spigot and wasting at the bung' in most people's ideas of economy. Some young spendthrifts will squander fifty dollars in winning the favor of a theatrical manager in order to get two complimentary passes to a play.

"In writing a letter, careful use of pen, ink, and paper, and particularly of words, is necessary. If you state what you have to say in a business letter clearly, in a single paragraph, if possible, you will earn the commendation and high esteem of the man to whom it is addressed. He will appreciate your consideration of him.

"As a man advances in life, he may extend his ventures into new fields until he reaches the apex of his mental and recuperative powers, when it is wisdom, thrift, economy, — what you will, — for him to concentrate his interests."

It is by the mysterious power of economy, it has been said, that the loaf is multiplied, that using does not waste, that little becomes much, that scattered fragments grow to unity, and that out of nothing or next to nothing comes the miracle of something. It is not merely saving, still less, parsimony. It is foresight and arrangement, insight and combination, causing inert things to labor, useless things to serve our necessities, perishing things to renew their vigor, and all things to exert themselves for human comfort.

"It is surprising how little it takes for the real necessaries of life," said Andrew Carnegie in the "Youth's Companion." "A little home paid for and a few thousand dollars — a very few, — make all the difference. These are more easily acquired by frugal people than you might suppose.

"Great wealth is quite another and a far less desirable matter. It is not the aim of thrift, or the duty of men, to acquire millions. It is in no respect a virtue to set this before us as an end. Duty to save ends when just enough money has been put aside to provide comfortably for those dependent upon us. Hoarding millions is avarice, not thrift.

"Of course, under our industrial conditions, it is inevitable that a few, a very few men, will find money coming to them far beyond their wants. There are men who have millions, and who continue to pursue money-making only to collect more millions for hoarding. This is, as I have said, a very different thing from thrift and the making of a modest competence. The accumulation of millions of dollars is usually the result of enterprise and judgment, and some exceptional ability for organization. It does not come from savings in the ordinary sense of that word. Men who in old age strive only to increase their already too great hoards are usually slaves of the habit of hoarding formed in their youth. At first they own the money they have made and saved. Later in life the money owns them, and they cannot help themselves, so overpowering is the force of habit, either for good or evil.

"It is the abuse of the civilized saving instinct, and not its use, that produces this class of men. No one need be afraid of falling a victim to this abuse of habit, if he always bears in mind that whatever surplus wealth may come to him is to be regarded as a sacred trust, which he is bound to administer for the good of his fellows.

"If a man resolves and faithfully adheres to his resolution never to hoard money, but to put each year's surplus to uses beneficial to others, then the money-making habit may still be classed among the virtues. The man must always be master. He should keep money in the position of a useful servant; he must never let it master and make a miser of him.

"Burns expresses a truth when he declares that savings are precious because they make a man independent. As he was a very poor man himself, to be independent of others naturally seemed to him the great aim of life; but great wealth is even more desirable, since it permits one to be of service to others."

"Provided he has some ability and good sense to start with, is thrifty, honest, and economical," said Philip D. Armour, "there is no reason why any young man should not accumulate money and attain so-called success in life." When asked to what qualities he attributed his own success, Mr. Armour said: "I think that thrift and economy had much to do with it. I owe much to my mother's training and to a good line of Scotch ancestors, who have always been thrifty and economical."

"Thrift is so essential to happiness in this world that the failure to practice it is to me incomprehensible," said Russell Sage, in the "Saturday Evening Post." "It is such an easy, simple thing, and it means so much. It is the foundation of success in business, of contentment in the home, of standing in society. It stimulates industry. I never yet heard of a thrifty man who was lazy. It begets independence and self-confidence. It makes a man of the individual who practices it.

"I think the greatest fault that characterizes our education of the young, to-day, is failure to teach thrift in the schools. From the very outset a child ought to understand the value of saving. In some schools, I understand, penny savings funds are now established. Out of these funds, if they are administered with practical common sense, will grow more sound teaching than out of anything else in the curriculum. I mean teaching that will make for success; and that, after all, is what the mother hopes for for her child and a nation for its citizens.

"As matters stand now, all that the average child ever hears in school of the value of saving is contained in some dry text-book or essay. There is nothing living, vital, or forcible in such material as this. It is of very much greater importance that a child or a young man should know how to proceed on the road to success in the world than it is that he should know the road to Cape Town or London, or that he should know the involved principles of the higher sciences.

"This is a very practical world, and the man is going to get the most out of it who is not hampered by a constant want of money. It is absurd to suppose that great riches always bring happiness, or even that the accumulation of great riches is essential to success. The man of moderate means is, on the whole, perhaps, happier than the extremely rich man, and he who makes for himself a safe place in any field can be set down as being quite as successful as the man who accumulates millions. But the man who is perpetually hard up cannot under any circumstances be happy, no matter what the foolish in the world may say; and no man can win a safe place in the world if he is hampered with debts. Helpless poverty is the most crushing affliction that can come to a family, and is the affliction most easily avoided. The man who starts out right will never be poor in the extreme sense, no matter how limited his income, or how circumscribed his opportunities.

"Let him lay down the rule for himself that he will invariably spend less than he makes; then he is safe. No man can be happy in this life, for any length of time, if he does not live up to this principle, no matter how dazzlingly he starts out, or what his prospects are. If he deviates from this rule, he will sooner or later come to grief. He must save to succeed. He must succeed in something to be happy. That man surely faces acute misery who at thirty is not better off than he was at twenty. It is a simple process, and for its non-observance there can be no possible excuse. Let the boy or man live so economically that he always has something to lay by, and he is certain to have, in the end, a competence to protect him against all ordinary worries. Of course, there may come unavoidable accidents; but even these will be more easily combated if, as a young man, a habit of economizing has been cultivated. I wonder constantly, when I meet examples of misery caused by unthriftiness, how such things can be with a human being whose brain is normal. Make it a rule to save at least twenty-five cents of every dollar you earn. Save seventy-five cents if you can, but never less than twenty-five."

"Those who really desire to attain independence," said P. T. Barnum, "have only to set their minds upon it and adopt the proper means, as they do in regard to any other object which they wish to accomplish, and the thing is easily done. But, however easy it may be found to make money, I have no doubt that many will agree that it is the most difficult thing in the world to keep it. The way to acquire a competence is to expend less than one earns, which seems a very simple problem. But you may say, 'I understand this; this is economy, and I know that economy is wealth; I know that I can't eat my cake and keep it also!' But I beg to say that, perhaps, more cases of failure arise from mistakes on this point than on almost any other. The fact is, many people think they understand economy when they really do not.

"True economy is misapprehended, and people go through life without properly comprehending what that principle is. Some say, 'I have an income of so much, and here is my neighbor who has the same; yet every year he gets something ahead, while I fall short; why is it? I know all about economy.' He thinks he does, but he does not. There are many who think that economy consists in saving cheese-parings and candle ends, in cutting off two cents from the laundress's bill, and in doing all sorts of little, mean, selfish things. Economy is not meanness. The misfortune is, also, that such persons let their economy apply in only one direction. They fancy they are so wonderfully economical in saving a half-penny, where they ought to spend twopence, that they think they can afford to squander in other directions. Before kerosene oil was discovered or thought of, for instance, one might stop over night at almost any farmer's house in the agricultural districts and get a very good supper, but after supper he might attempt to read in the sitting room, and would find it difficult with the insufficient light of a single candle. The hostess, seeing his dilemma, would say: 'It is rather hard to read here evenings; the proverb says, "You must have a ship at sea in order to be able to burn two candles at once;" we never have an extra candle except on extra occasions.' These extra occasions would occur, perhaps, twice a year. In this way the good woman would save five, six, or ten dollars annually; but the information which might have been derived from having the extra light, of course, would have outweighed a ton of candles.

"But the trouble did not end there. Feeling that she was so economical in tallow candles, she would think she could afford to go frequently to the village, and spend twenty or thirty dollars a year for ribbons and furbelows, many of which were not necessary. This false economy may frequently be seen in men of business, and in those instances it often runs to writing paper. You will find good business men who save all their old envelopes and scraps, and would not tear a new sheet of paper, if they could avoid it, for the world. This is all very well; they may in this way save five or ten dollars a year; but, being so economical, (only in note paper,) they think they can afford to waste time, to have expensive parties, and to drive their carriages. I never knew a man to succeed by practicing this kind of economy.

"True economy consists in always making the income exceed the outgo. Wear the old clothes a little longer, if necessary; dispense with the new pair of gloves; mend the old dress; live on plainer food, if need be; so that, under all circumstances, unless some unforeseen accident occurs, there will be a margin in favor of the income. A penny here, and a dollar there, placed on interest, go on accumulating, and in this way the desired result is attained. It requires some training, perhaps, to accomplish this economy; but, when once used to it, you will find there is more satisfaction in rational saving than in irrational spending. Here is a recipe which I recommend, for I have found it to work an excellent cure for extravagance, and especially for mistaken economy: When you find that you have no surplus at the end of the year, and yet have a good income, I advise you to take a few sheets of paper and form them into a book and mark down every item of expenditure. Post it every day or week in two columns, one headed 'necessaries,' or even 'comforts,' and the other headed 'luxuries,' and you will find that the latter column will be double, treble, and frequently ten times as great as the former. The real comforts of life cost but a small portion of what most of us can earn. It is the fear of what Mrs. Grundy may say that keeps the noses of many worthy families to the grindstone."

Very few men know how to use money properly. They can earn it, lavish it, hoard it, waste it; but to deal with it *wisely*, as a means to an end, is an education difficult of acquirement.

NATURE IS LIBERAL, NOT LAVISH.

"Nature uses a grinding economy," says Emerson, "working up all that is wasted to-day into to-morrow's creation; not a superfluous grain of sand for all the ostentation she makes of expense and public works. She flung us out in her plenty, but we cannot shed a hair or a paring of a nail, but instantly she snatches at the shred and appropriates it to her general stock." Last summer's flowers and foliage decayed in autumn only to enrich the earth this year for other forms of beauty. Nature will not even wait for our friends to see us, unless we die at home. The moment the breath has left the body, she begins to take us to pieces, that the parts may be used again for other creations.

Liberal, not lavish, is Nature's hand. Even God, it is said, cannot afford to be extravagant. When He increased the loaves and fishes, he commanded to gather up the fragments, that nothing be lost.

To find out uses for the persons or things which are

now wasted in life is to be the glorious work of the men of the next generation, and that which will contribute most to their enrichment.

> Rarely they rise by virtue's aid who be
> Plunged in the depth of helpless poverty.
>
> *Dryden.*

Frugality may be termed the daughter of Prudence, the sister of Temperance, the parent of Liberty. He that is extravagant will quickly become poor, and poverty will enforce dependence and invite corruption. — *Samuel Johnson.*

I once knew a very covetous, sordid fellow, who used to say: "Take care of the pence, for the pounds will take care of themselves." — *Chesterfield.*

There are but two ways of paying debt: increase of industry in raising income, and increase of thrift in laying it out. — *Carlyle.*

There is no royal road to wealth, any more than there is to learning. It costs hard work, and the relinquishment of many pleasures, and most men may have it who will pay the price. — *J. G. Holland.*

Economy is half the battle of life. — *C. H. Spurgeon.*

Riches amassed in haste will diminish; but those collected by hand, and little by little, will multiply. — *Goethe.*

> To catch Dame Fortune's golden smile,
>   Assiduous wait upon her;
> An' gather gear by every wile
>   That's justified by honor:
> Not for to hide it in a hedge,
>   Nor for a train-attendant,
> But for the glorious privilege
>   Of being independent.
>
> *Burns.*

> For age and want save while you may;
> No morning sun lasts a whole day.
>
> *Franklin.*

Printed in the United States
38963LVS00006B/20